Contents

When I was nine, I went to work in London.

wooden house

2

The streets of London were narrow
and smelly.

One night, at the end of that hot summer,
I heard shouting outside.

A fire had started in a baker's shop.

The fire started in a baker's shop in Pudding Lane on 2 September 1666.

I ran up to my master's room.

Houses were built mainly of wood with thatched roofs and they caught fire easily.

6

Houses and shops nearby were on fire.

7

We ran out on to the street.

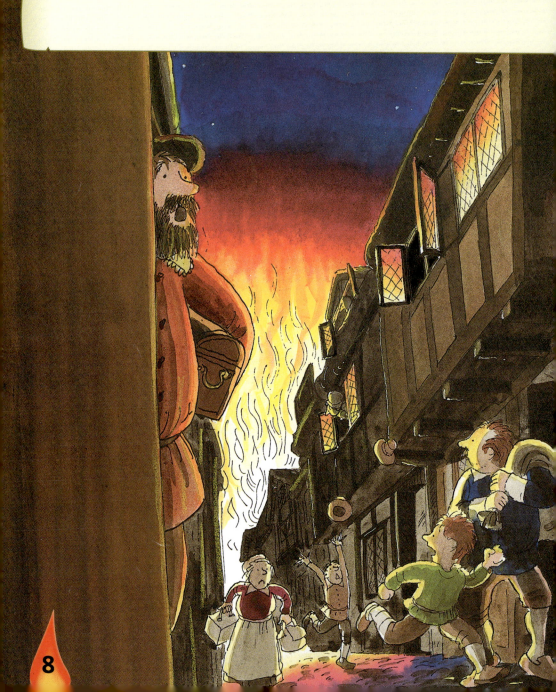

It was a windy night.
The wind blew the flames.

Fire spread down
Pudding Lane to
warehouses where oil
and spirits were stored.

9

We joined people who were running away.

Some people tried to put out the flames.

There were no fire engines, so they used axes and fire hooks to pull down burning buildings.

fire hooks

We ran down to the river.

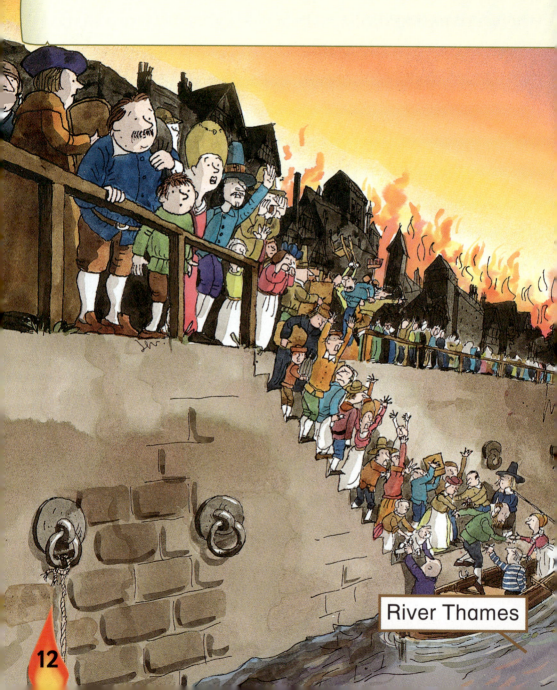

River Thames

Boats were taking people across the river.

London Bridge

There was no room for us.

The fire spread to London Bridge.

A gap caused by a fire in 1633, stopped the fire spreading across the bridge.

We went to help put out the flames.

People made a chain to work together.

We worked all night.

Water had to be carried from the river.

We saw houses being blown up
to try to stop the fire.

But the fires kept burning.

On the evening of the fourth day, the fire was at last put out.

We were happy to be alive.

The Great Fire of London destroyed 1,300 houses and 87 churches.

Index